Meditate

Emily Woosley

BookLeaf Publishing

India | USA | UK

Presentation by *BookLeaf Publishing*

Web: www.bookleafpub.com

E-mail: info@bookleafpub.com

ISBN: 9789363319141

First edition 2024

For You.

PREFACE

It was crucial to me that this collection be entirely my own words.

Encore

I delivered my lines just like rehearsed.
My body threatened to fail me,
My voice shaky, but convincing.
I delivered the performance of a lifetime,
While I could still feel your knife between my
thighs.
It took time to find my voice strong enough
to put on another show.
This time, I was the director.
My body did not fail me,
My voice, loud and proud.
They pulled the rope for my curtain call.
Yours, they had to cut from the raptors.
I will have an encore.

Calling For You

With clenched fists,
I wait for him to finish,
Diving as far into me as he can.
He's trying to force his name onto my lips.
But the only name that threatens to escape,
Is yours.

Wake Me Up

You left before I woke.
I wanted to tell myself I was relieved.
But if I'm being honest,
It was as if my whole body
Disappeared into the mattress
And it would take a million "hellos",
To pull me back out from the place
Your nonexistent goodbye put me.

Unwanted

I've had men want me so badly,
That they'll find any possible way to have me.
In a car, on a dark street,
Or in a nearby nook.
But I've never had a man want me so badly,
That a car wasn't a suitable enough location.

Unspeakable

5

She would not say it's name.
To name such things,
Was to give them power.
And yet, it was impossible
To keep her mind from whispering.

Scars

I existed before you.
Right?
I had to, I see the scars.
But I no longer feel the pain.
For the first time in my life,
I'm no longer existing.
I am living.

Homesick

From the moment I met you...
There was an emptiness
when you weren't near me.
At first I couldn't place it.
Until one day,
The moment we parted,
I realized,
I was homesick.

Did Yours Feel Like This?

I all but laughed in your face
when you told me you had made love.
"Is that a fancy way to say you got fucked?"
Oh how I wish I could tell you.
I wish I could tell you about how I hid my
embarrassment as tears fell involuntarily from
my eyes as they held me.
"It's okay Baby, it's just love."
That's what my ears heard.
But my heart,
My heart must've heard all the words that had
never been spoken in my presence before.
I made love in that moment.
My heart, made love.
I'm sorry I can't tell you I'm sorry.

Somebody

I used to see you from time to time.
It had been a while,
But I caught a glimpse.
"What's your name?"
But you quickly turned
and you were gone.
You looked so sad.
"Come back, let me help you."
You came back.
"I've missed you."
"I've been here."
"You look pretty."
"I look old."
"I like your dress."
"I look too fat in this."
"Whats your name?"
"I'm nobody."
I tried to tell you how beautiful you were,
And that you were somebody to me.
But you wouldn't listen.
I left, feeling defeated.
I couldn't get you off my mind.
Why didn't you listen?
Why did you look so sad? Couldn't you see?
Walking home, I passed a shop.

I turned to take a glance.
I saw you there, once again.
You moved when I moved,
You spoke when I spoke.
"You look beautiful today."
"So do you."
And for a second,
I saw us smile.

Wings

If you had given me a chance,
I could've flown.
With a little encouragement,
You could've thrown me into the air
And watched me soar.
Instead, you threw me into the water,
And turned your back while I drowned.

Emily

I searched for it.
I listened closely.
I heard whispers
and I heard screams.
But I never heard it.
I knew what he called me couldn't be right.
Surely it was something softer,
Something sweeter.
Then, I heard you.
You didn't yell, you didn't whisper.
You looked into my eyes,
And into my soul.
And for the first time I could remember,
I heard my name.

Please

I stood alone with my shovel,
Though a circle of people surrounded me.
I called for you.
For anyone to help.
"He's here. Why won't you help me?"
I begged you for help.
You made me bury him alone.

Stormy Weather

There has always been a storm brewing inside
me.
Lightening and claps of thunder would jar me
awake.
Tornadoes would rip apart my relationships
before they even started.
Floods would come in waves when no one else
was around.
But you, Darling.
You show me the beauty in the storm.
You show me the calm before and after.
The smell that tickles your senses in the best
way.
The way the sky lights up or the electricity you
can feel in your bones.
You never tried to stop my storm...
You just showed me how to dance in the rain.

Tears

You don't deserve my tears.
I feel the heat on my cheeks.
The water beginning to rise in my eyes.
But I don't give in.
I won't give you that power.
The power to know I cry for you.
That not only sticks and stones break my bones
But the words do hurt me.
I will not let you see my tears.
The warm water in my face
Will wash away the evidence before you realize.
The drain, carrying away the tears you caused.
But you, you will not know I cry for you.
The shower walls will tell you nothing.

They Tell Me

Today's pain will be tomorrows ache.
Tomorrows ache will be next weeks sting.
But eventually, the pain,
Will be only a memory.
But today,
Tomorrow seems so far away.

Kiss of Death

I told you,
I could do one or the other
You begged and pleaded
Until I gave in
and laid down for you
I knew it was over as you ripped the foil open
You asked me not to run
But we both knew I'd never be back

Cutting

I look down and see the blood.
A fresh cut.
I told myself I would stop this madness.
I see too many scars.
I shake my head and close my eyes.
When I open,
The blood is gone.
The scars never existed.
How long will my imagination be enough?

RIP

I've never mourned the loss of anyone
Except myself.
Its a weird sensation.
Mourning so deeply,
the loss of someone,
you barely knew

Hate

I think I gathered hatred at a young age.
I can't explain why I feel like I had it,
Waiting for someone to receive it.
I didn't have to wait long
Until my hate found an outlet.
I hated hard and I hated well.
I hated him for most of my life.
When he took his own life,
My hatred scattered.
I felt empty and I felt I had a choice.
Pick up the hatred yet again, or let it lie.
I chose to let it stay amongst the dust of his
ashes.
Instead I picked up every emotion I had not
become accustomed to.
I picked up contentment, and jealousy.
I picked up fear and I picked up happiness.
I had to learn to live without this piece of me I
had carried so long.
I didn't know if I could survive it,
Feeling everything new and foreign,
Until I learned how to use the last thing I picked
up.
Love.

Heavy

I can't hold my head up.
My mind is too heavy.
My thoughts too messy.
I can hear them.
I can see them.
But I can't share them.
I've learned my lesson.
I hate to be a bother.
But could I rest my head
On your shoulder if I promise
Not to cry.

Anger

I thought we parted ways,
You and I.
It was nasty,
But needed.
Why are you here
Unannounced and loud.
With you, came all the old feelings.
Are you proud of yourself?